How To Score With A Girl, By A Girl
...Advice for Men

The Guide Book,
Quick, Informative and Funny

By Amy Ashton

To all the Men that had me at "hello"
...and then kept talking.

Author, Amy Ashton is a professional Stand-Up Comedienne, Host and Executive Producer.

Chosen by Mitzi Shore to develop her stand up act, she became a favorite at **The World Famous Comedy Store**. Although sometimes having to follow acts on stage like **Chris Rock**, **Dice Clay**, **Eddie Griffin** etc, and having to hang with a lot of testosterone her quick sarcastic wit became a way of survival along with constantly giving relationship advice to her male comic friends. They would say to her, "Girl you should be charging for this." And so Amy started including her expertise in her act when she traveled the country performing especially at Universities, and they drank it up.

She has been a successful consultant for many singles guys including one of the Bachelor's that won the title, "America's Most Eligible Bachelor" on **NBC's EXTRA** as well as married guys needing to re-connect.

She is now an Executive Producer of TV Shows she Created that aired on **E!** Network as well as continually writes and produces Health and Beauty Specials and is a Host/Bitch coach of another show she created, *Anything But Plastic as* well hosts MTV's, *Celeb Red Carpet Interviews*.

She continues her comedy at Clubs, Colleges, Corporate events and produces the Comedy Show, Comedy Angels Live, Still Singe Tour. And you may have seen her in one her many National commercials.

Wow, why doesn't she just write a book? Oh, yeah she did. *How to Score With a Girl, By a Girl.*

Amy Ashton

For Copies, Bookings or Advice go to
www.amyashton.com/book.htm

or contact at HowToScore@aol.com

Contents

Introduction

What? *How to score with a girl?* I don't need this book!"

"I'm rich and handsome."

"I'm charming and a natural comedian."

"I'm artistic and sexy."

Yeah, right... that is exactly *why* I wrote this book:

For all the times I found myself painfully attracted to the guys like the above, and wanted them to score with me. "They had me at "hello," and then struck out! So let me tell you guys, you need this book.

And for the ladies because we as women just expect you guys to be psychic and know the perfect thing to say to us. If we have to explain and actually tell you what we want, it takes all the romance out of it. Well now, ladies, finally there is someone to say it for you...me!

Guys, I'll be answering a lot of questions you wanted to know but were afraid to ask women. I interviewed many men and asked them,"If you were a fly on the wall in a room full of 'hotties' which question would you most like answered?" The following are the top three questions....

#1) Do girls really know if they are going to have sex with you in the first five minutes of meeting you?

#2) What is the fastest way to score?

#3) Does size really matter?

#1) Do girls really know if they are going to sleep with you in the first five minutes?

Five minutes? That's a long time; you could have talked yourself out of it by then. The answer is, yes. Girls usually know if we are attracted to you in the first few seconds and then we put you through a test period. When I meet a guy I find myself attracted to it's as if the game show "Family Feud" goes through my head: three wrong answers and you're out! I actually see the "X"'s and hear the loud buzzer.

This is one of the reasons I wrote this book: Every girl scores you with a check list and I'm here to help you get a home run.

#2) What's the fastest way to score? And
#3) Does size really matter?

Patience, I'll get to those questions later in the book.

(Yeah, I know sometimes I can be a *tease*.)

And taking into consideration that you guys want to *score fast*, I wrote in easy to read formats...

Example: "Question/Multiple Choice," because I know men won't want to read *whole* paragraphs. In fact I change formats with each chapter because I know how you guys love *variety*.

Chapter 1

Score Faster

Get in the game. This covers how to connect and get a girl to give you a chance.

Question 1:

What is a clever way to get a girls phone number?

    a) Car accident

    b) Ask her help because you lost your cell phone and need her to call it, so you can find it.

    c) Tell her you don't need it because you'll be outside her window.

Answer to Question 1:

b) "Help, I lost my cell phone."

Comments: This is the least likely to get you arrested.

Comments on wrong answers:.

a) Car accident. If you can avoid being involved in the car accident, even better! Instead stage it and just act as the "witness." I found out a guy did that to me. I appreciated him going the extra mile. Any guy can just ask for the date...boring.

c) *Tell her you don't need it because you'll be outside her window.* Unfortunately I had a guy do that as well. I got to a point I was going to have to get a restraining order but they cost $500 dollars and the gun was only $150. And that you can use over and over again. (Just clean it with each new relationship.)

Question 2:

Which is more likely to help you score when going out on the town?

a) Go out on the town with your best-looking buddy to act as a wingman.

b) Make sure you show up with a pack of your guy friends so she can see how popular you are.

c) A few friends but most importantly don't forget at least one female wingman.

(And TWO Wingers are better than one)

Answer to Question 2:

c) Don't forget a female wingman!

Comments: Girls like another attractive woman giving the "ok" for a guy. It's sort of like a professional referral. This is a great way to rack up points fast.

Question 3:

You're at a bar and there *she* is, your dream girl. She is huddled with her thirsty friends, do you...

a) Wait for her to approach you? After all you are God's gift to women.

b) Introduce yourself to her and see if she seems *responsive?* Give her a poke... LOL, I mean compliment. Offer to buy her a drink, and possibly her thirsty friends as well, but make sure your focus is only on her.

 c) Flirt with one of her friends to make the bitch jealous.

Answer to Question 3:

b) Give her a compliment. Offer to buy her a drink.

Comments: Guys, try to look at it like going to Vegas, you're going to throw down some extra money for entertainment and gambling. Roll the dice on an actual person and see if one will roll over for you. You'll have more of a chance than strip clubs and porn.

Comments on wrong answers:

a) Wait for her to approach you?

Strike, unless you're Brad Pitt. Know your category and stay in your lane.

c) Flirt with one of her friends?

This is very important **not** to do. Girls like to be "**the**" girl not "**a**" girl. Unlike most men who accept almost anywhere or anyone to scrape their rocket.

Question 4:

Which of the following is the best opening line or ice breaker?

a) Want to go out? I drive a Porsche.

b) Wow, you must sleep in Tupperware because you are fresh.

c) You have a beautiful smile.

d) I'm looking for someone to marry, and financially support.

(Thank God for Tennis shoes, because you never know when you'll have to get away fast!)

Answer to Question 4:

d) I'm looking for someone to marry, and financially support.

Comments: LOL. It's a good one but you better have a back-up plan or you're Tennies. ("I said I was looking for MARY not someone to marry.") I know a Doctor that does this and he could wall paper his High-rise with all the girls that would like to shoot him in the head.

And also c) You have a beautiful smile.
Comments: Here it is on a platter and it's FREE and no need to worry about get-away plan! Just give her a compliment. That's it! The key is to make the girl feel good about herself

Comments on wrong answers:

a) "Want to go out? I drive a Porsche."...So, are you going to give it to her? Who cares? In LA if a guy drives a Porsche, he probably lives in it, and can't afford a beer. Most likely his license plate is his ZIP code.

b) "You must sleep in Tupperware..."

Oh yeah baby, nothing like corny humor to make a girl spread her legs.

Question 5:

How do I get a successful conversation going?

a) Try to find something that you have in common.

b) Complain to her about how you just dumped your psycho ex.

c) Make fun of the people around you.

Answer to Question 5:

a) Try to find something in common that you agree on.

Comments: Find out what she likes to do. Perhaps a movie she wants to see or her favorite restaurant. This isn't the time for you to argue and be "right."

Comments on wrong answers:

b) Double strike on complaining and telling her about how you just dumped your psycho "ex." Once, a cop offered to buy me a drink as he was complaining about his "psycho ex-girlfriend." Yeah, right on, I really need a guy in my life that hates women, has a gun in his pocket **and** the *law* on his side.

c) Make fun of people. Keep the conversation positive. Try not to say anything negative at all. "The loose sexy woman," behind the bar," might be her Mother and the "One-eyed biker chick" her sister. Oops!

Question 6:

You are standing at a crosswalk/stoplight waiting for the light to change and there "she" is. Do you...

a) Stay on your cell phone to show how cool you are?

b) Bring up something common, like the traffic you are waiting for, and if she responds continue to engage in conversation?

c) Ignore her, wait until she is so far away she can barely hear you, and then yell at her, "Hey, want to go out some time?"

d) She doesn't seem responsive so call her a c@nt and walk away.

Answer to Question 6:

b) Bring up something common, and if she responds continue to engage in conversation.

Comments: A score for striking while the iron is hot.

Comments on wrong answers:

c) Wait until she is so far away she can barely hear you, and then yell at her," (Hot guy, but unfortunately he did this. LOL, did he expect me to run back across the street to him?)

a) Stay on phone. STRIKE

d) She doesn't seem responsive so call her a "c@nt" and walk away. Yeah right, that should work.

Question 7:

How do you ask for the date?

a) Find out what she would like to do, and then ask her if she would like to do one of those specific things.

b) Be general. Say something like, "want to hang sometime and then fool around?"

c) Just get her phone number. You can always ask her out another time, and that way you won't get rejected.

Answer to Question 7:

a) SCORE! *Find out a specific thing she would like to do.*

Comments: Just like your mind is on sex, her mind will be on the "fun thing" you are doing together. It will take a lot of pressure off you and possibly give you a chance. This is how girls think, and it's the best way to get her to give you a chance. I mean to get in her pants.

Comments on wrong answers: *b) Want to hang some time and then fool around?* No joking about sex. Always act/pretend to be gracious even if sex is the only reason you listen to her gab. Hide that at all times. This will help you score a lot faster.

c) Just get her phone number. You can always ask her out another time.

Strike! LOSER!

Question 8:

I've got her number! How long should I wait to make the "call" for the actual date?

a) Three days. That's the rule.

b) Next day.

c) Ask as you're getting her number.

Answer to Question 8:

c) Ask as you're getting her number.

Comments: (Unless she is willing to make the date plans on the spot.) It was one of the best ways a guy asked me out. No games. After he got my phone number, he said, "OK, now would you like me to call you tomorrow, wait three days, or call Monday and see when you have some time? It was disarming. Be gracious, guys. It will save you a lot of time and money.

Comments on wrong answers:

a) *Three days.* This could cause her to blow you off (instead of you). Instead make her feel she is special without coming across desperate. This is about you scoring as fast as possible not who has the power.

b) *Next day.* Could be okay, but c) is better.

Question 9:

<u>How</u> **do you contact her to ask her out?**

a) Text her. "Hi babe it's me, the Millionaire. Call me back. I'll be in town next week. I'd like to take you out."

b) Leave phone message, "Hi beautiful, this is Greg. I can't get you off my mind. You haven't returned my call, and now every time I pass Gelsons where we first met I want to cry."

c) Leave a phone message, "Hi, it's Greg. I met you at Jen's party last Saturday. My phone number is ....Please give me a call when you get a minute or I will try you back another time."

d) Text her a picture your private parts.

Answer to Question 9:

c) "Hi, this is Greg. I met you at Jen's party last Saturday..."

Comments: Be polite and leave *all* the facts like your name, where and when you met.

Comments on wrong answers:

a) Text her. "Hi babe it's me, the Millionaire call me back. I'll be in town next week. I'd like to take you out." This is a great way to attract dumb gold-diggers. Personally I wouldn't respond to a text at all, but hey, it did work for a famous Pro-Golfer and all his whores. Also the text he sent is not specific or classy. This guy probably sent it out to twenty girls as well.

b) Every time I pass the Supermarket I cry. Hey Greg, next time you're at the Supermarket *crying*, pick up some tampons... for yourself.

d) Text her a picture your private parts

Jewelry yes, "private parts" NO, unless you're trying to get a date with Richard Simmons.

Question 10:

What's the best way of suggesting to get to the first date?

a) Say "Hey, I'll go to your place or you can come to mine, and then we'll decide what we'll do...if you know what I mean."

b) Ask her, would she feel more comfortable if you pick her up or meet at the destination.

c) Tell her to pick you up because your Maserati is in the shop now.

Answer to Question:10

b) Ask her if she'd feel more comfortable if you pick her up or meet at the destination.

Comments: "Comfortable" is the key word here so she trusts you. You are a stranger to her at this point, but if you don't want to be one for long always try to make her feel comfortable and that you are a safe person to be around.

Comments on wrong answers:

a) "I'll go to your place or you'll come to mine. We'll decide what to do if you know what I mean." Sounds like a date with Mike Tyson.

c) My Maserati is in the shop now.

Saying you have a Maserati when you don't is almost as bad as, after you spent all your rent money on dinner, finding out she used to be a man.

Question 11:

What should I talk about on the first date?

a) Positive fun things

b) Your psycho exes, or evil mother.

c) Her, unless she starts talking about how fascinating her cats are.

Answer to Question 11

a) *Talk about positive fun things.*

Comments: Try to find out what you have in common. Perhaps prepare an interesting story to share.

Comments on wrong answers:

b) *On a date talk about* your *psycho exes or evil mother.*

Here is some advice worth a lot of money. I should be charging for this (oh, yeah, I am). All a girl has to do is ask you how you feel about your mother and she will know your whole future. Don't "mother bash" or again, "ex bash". She will think that is going to be her. If you hate your mother, hide that.

c) *Act like you're interested in those fascinating cat stories.*   Ouch, I know this is painful, but if you have a date with a girl who looks like Megan Fox and want to lie on top of her just like her cat does, just smile and think about how she'll look naked.

Question 12:

Who pays for the first date?

a) We go Dutch.

b) She offered, so I won't argue.

c) The guy.

Answer To Question 12:

a) *The guy!* Comments: Do you ever want to score with this girl (or one of her "hot friends...shhh)? I know it seems unfair, but it's just the way it is; and besides, girls spend a lot of money on clothes, lipstick and getting their hair done (so actually you owe us money).

Comments on wrong answers:

b) *We go dutch and c) She offered I won't argue.*

Don't fall for this. Always insist on paying. Kind of like if you cheated on her and offered to cut off a finger, you wouldn't want her to take you up on that would you? Well SAME thing as letting her pay. Another, piece of advice, if you're going to be the

"Big man" and pay for the whole dinner then don't forget to pay for the valet. If you do, you might as well go Dutch, and no need to have broken out the clean underwear for the evening.

Question 13:

What do I do if a girl asks me to pay for her rent before the salad comes?

a) Unless you looked this girl up in the yellow pages under, "prostitute," gets up and leave

b) Blow it off. She was just kidding, and besides she is hot and you like a good trade.

c) Immediately take out your check book.

Answer to Question 13:

a) Unless you looked this girl up in the yellow pages under "prostitute," get up and leave! Comments: Don't waste your time! She is not going to change.

Comments on wrong answers:

b) She was just kidding, and besides she's "hot." OK, that could be an option, but then realize some guys ignore the signs right in the beginning, and then when the girl dumps them they say, "All girls are gold diggers." No, *you* like all girls who are gold diggers.

c) Take out your check book. You can find prostitutes on line now. It's called "Millionaire Match.com." It's for a bunch of "actresses." Yeah, they *act* like they don't want your money. I always wondered what kind of guys would want you to want them for their money. Evidently, extremely fat men. My girlfriend tried the site. She said Mr. Hefty showed up but with some nice Manolo Boots from Neiman Marcus for her.

Question 14:

How do I know if she wants sex?

a) Right away. If I'm f@@king horny, she must be.

b) When her hand is on your crotch that is safe inclination.

c) After I've spent "x" amount of money on her. I'm not into gold diggers.

Answer To Question 14:

b) When her hand is on your crotch that is safe inclination.

Comments: I know you guys like to put a time limit on it. HIDE that.

Comments on wrong answers:

a) Right away. If I'm f@@king horny, she must be. FYI, that's called rape.

c) After I've spent "x" amount of money on her. I'm not into gold diggers.

Then sharpen your skills, slugger, OR put an ad on Craig's List. "Yeah I'm looking for a blonde that can suck my di@k into a new country for... $25.00 bucks, please."

Chapter 2:

Know Your Category and Stay In Your Lane

How to Score With a Girl, By a Girl

Find your category...

Hot Guy

Hunky Guy with a Heart

Sensitive Artist Type

Rich Guy

Rich and Handsome

Playboy

Attractive and wants a relationship

Lonely Loser

Smart and Sensitive

Funny and fat

Funny and charming

Technical genius

Hot and broke

Broke and ugly

Powerful and ugly

Handsome, rich

A$$hole

Know Your Category and Stay In Your Lane

What are you fishing for?

22-year-old petite stuck up blonde

Young, cute, low self-esteem

MILF

Manipulative hot chick

Mysterious hard to get

Attractive and sweet

Shy girl

Aggressive woman

Gold digger

Middle aged, hot and easy

Hot and a challenge

Super BITCH

Loose and easy

Intelligent and horny

Horny

Technical genius

Charming and funny

Find your category. If you don't know ask three of your friends. I'm sure they will be thrilled to enlighten you. Honesty hurts but saves you time and money.

If the girl of your dreams seems "materialistic" and only dates "rich guys" and you are not, you can...

Lesson #1

Be creative and find **another way** of getting it.

Example:

Guys assume I'm only impressed with a rich guy who will *buy* me something. So not true. I'd like a guy... to *steal* me something (then return it, then buy it).

Now that's hot! Go the extra mile. Show you care. Any guy can just "buy" you something. Seriously though, I am not condoning stealing. I am saying get creative guys! If you don't personally have what she wants but can still get it for her, you are in. (Maybe someone owes you a favor?)

Lesson #2

Be aware **of selling** yourself as a **"category" you are NOT,** only to be insulted when she rejects you for not living up to it.

Example: Category: **"Unattractive Sleazy Producer"**

doesn't equal

"Hot Irresistible 'Hunk with a Heart!'"

(Celebrity Interviews from Pre-MTV TV Awards)

If you're an unattractive sleazy "Powerful Guy" **playing** the "power card" and instead you rudely think I'm going to put out on the first date for a couple of $60.00 crab cakes you are SOL, LOL. Don't insult yourself or me, please. **Know your category and STAY IN YOUR LANE**. At least offer a couple shots to help ease the pain. Dude, DON'T switch lanes without signaling and think you are Brad Pitt or George Clooney (Hot Hunk Type).

Yo, Creepy Guy you are going to have to throw out a bone (or Guest Starring Role on sit-com you say you "write" for, lol). Do a sit- up. There is no room for resting on *your* laurels or cane. In fact save a lot of time, flip open the yellow pages, look under the heading "Escorts" and I'm sure you'll find a prostitute who will find you irresistible on the first "date."

Lesson #3

If you try **hooking her with something she's not into**, be prepared to **sell** her on something else.

Example:

The cashier at an ARCO gas station offered me gum and then tells me "he wants to connect with me."

What do I look like, a gum whore! At least throw in an apple pie. I have standards!"

"I'll tell you what, gas is so expensive if you fill my tank up I'll rub that dot off your head. **Know your category and stay in your lane!**

In other words, if you are going to lie to get a girl, be good at it OR get creative by selling her on something else... other than gum or crab cakes!

Lesson #4

Just like cars, girl **"types"** come in different **packages**.

Example:

My friend Mark, a Loan Agent at my bank who wants to sell me a car loan, is "Charming Funny" guy. He says he is fishing for "22-year-old sexy blonde." I explained to him they come in different "packages" like a car. You may have to go with **Low Self Esteem** "22-Year-Old Hot blonde" model and then you can use your charm and humor to cheer her up. Your Boss with the hefty salary is probably screwing the **Hot Stuck- Up** "22-Year-Old Blonde" model... Oh wait, that is his Boss!

Chapter 3:

Men Are From Earth And Women Are Crazy!

Hello Amy, HELP ME READ THE SIGNS

Dave says, "Hello, Amy Help Me Read the Signs"

"Amy, I'm in love with this hot bartender chick. I like her as much as my hairdresser. You know the one that always flakes on me. Anyway, I think the bartender is interested. How should I go about asking her out?"

Men Are From Earth And Women Are Crazy!

Amy says, "Don't.

Instead find a girl who is acts nice to you, with a job that doesn't depend on you giving her money.

BUT if you insist on going for this one, toss out something you know she can't pass up. Most every girl I know is a sushi whore. Hey, maybe she'll down enough sake and sleep with you"

Comments: Another one that's going to ask me, "Why are all girls gold diggers?" Well I have a question for him. Let's say it together guys... "Why is it that all the women YOU like are gold diggers? "

BTW, he ended up marrying a Mail-Order

Bride. For the wedding, he asked everyone instead of gifts to please give cash... to go towards payment for her.

Great example of Chapter: *Know Your Category and Stay in Your Lane*, **Lesson #1**

"Be creative and find **another way** of getting it."

I am teaching you Guys skills!

Jerry, says, "Hello, Amy Help Me Read the Signs."

"Amy, it's my first day I just stared a new job. My boss is a bitch. I need her 'ok' on an upcoming project that will make the company a lot of money. I think she is on a power trip. I believe she purposely won't put it through because it's my idea. This pisses me off! Help! "

Amy says, "Hey Jerry,

It's your **first** day, they want you to work at the company, not run it. *Know your category and stay in your lane or* job description. Like it or not, it sounds like you actually need this lady. Why don't you just let the 'bitch' feel you respect her power since evidently she has it? The most important thing here is to get you what you want to make her feel it's her decision." (And then you can take her down later).

Richard says, "Hello, Amy Help Me Read the Signs."

"I met this cute lady at the dog park. She smiled at me first. We had a great conversation. At the end of the conversation I asked her if she would like to go hiking together. I waited a couple days and emailed her. I said, 'Hi, I'm Richard, the guy you met in the dog park. We talked about going hiking. Well I was thinking, we could go hiking, or for a nice dinner or just listen to some nice music.'

"She emailed me back and said, I wasn't clear in my email if I wanted to go as 'friends' or on a 'date.' Well, I was so insulted because I just wanted to go out and see what happens."

Men Are From Earth And Women Are Crazy!

Amy says, "Hey Richard, take a hike...by yourself."
You skipped ahead too fast for her. If you are
going to change lanes, signal first.

"She said she wanted to go 'hiking'. You had your
foot in the door. You should have gone hiking and
then *"see what happens'* as you say."

**Don't be caught being a W.L.L. (whining-lying-
loser) STRIKE!**

Chapter 4:

Hints for Scoring Girls on the Internet

Hints for Scoring Girls on the Internet

OK, so as far as "**Dating-sites**" and **Social Networking,** they could be a whole other book on they're own.

This book is more about connecting once you have met the girl so you can score.

However, I have comments for you since Internet Dating is soooo popular. I hear one out of five relationships start on the internet.

Give on-line correspondence a TIME LIMIT to get to the first date. Don't waste weeks of your time bull-shitting online with some con-artist just to finally meet the 500 pound girl that uses pictures of herself from eight years ago.

Or OMG you find out it's actually Jimmy from Nigeria who just needed you to wire all your money.

Hints for Scoring Girls on the Internet

The internet is a **great filter for rejection**. In everyday life average-looking Bill tells me he has to constantly face rejection, unlike on-line where only the girls that could tolerate his look responded, and so he happily avoided unnecessary rejection.

When he met the girls, he applied my lessons from this book, *How to Score With A Girl, By A Girl,* and got multiple home runs with multiple girls. (Note: Just don't forget to use a glove. He is now a proud father!)

Advertisements to attract girls on online:

I know one guy that attracts a lot of girls and is extremely successful by including the following buzz words or statements in his ad like how he is **"caring, protective, owns real-estate, and that he loves to shop."**

Hints for Scoring Girls on the Internet

I know another "Gentleman" that put an ad up saying **"Business owner looking for an *Assistant*."**

You'll be "interviewing" all week.

Note: I am not recommending, just reporting. AND **prepare well** for "hook and **sell something else**" (last Chapter, *Know your Category* **Lesson #3**).

Another way to attract Gold Diggers that you can complain about later...

A guy friend of mine was sickly upset when he found out his ex girlfriend dumped him for an ad a guy twittered,"I'm a TV Executive and the first girl who can guess who I am gets $1000." Fifty girls showed up for him to choose from. (Only dumb Gold-diggers need reply.)

Hints for Scoring Girls on the Internet

As you continue to the next chapter, you will see I give you plenty of places to meet and approach LIVE women. Come on sluggers; let's see if you can step up to the plate.

(Someone else can write the books, "Sex from Social Networking," "How I Saw Tits from Twitter," or "F@cks from Facebook").

Chapter 5:

Free Places to Meet LIVE Woman

The Supermarket

Comments:

Once I was standing by the spaghetti. A guy asked me, "When cooking spaghetti, how do you know when it's ready?" I told him," usually when my smoke alarm goes off. It's a good clue."

Then he said, "Since neither of us can cook how about I take you to Koi (popular LA restaurant)?"

Salsa Dancing

Comments:

I have a friend who is a Top Model. I went with her once to an event with a group of her "dancing friends" she met at class. I could not believe the dweebs that got to dance with her just because they were "great dancers."

Even if the guy is a troll, *if* he can move like a ride at Disneyland he is sooo in. This is a chance to get close to women you would never normally get a glance from. Truly AMAZING.

Alcohol Anonymous Recovery meeting

Free Places to Meet LIVE Woman

Comments:

Most women here seem to have very low self-esteem; they are accessible AND look at all the money you will save on not having to buy them drinks!

Church, Temple or spiritual awakening venue

Comments:

Just don't scream out to her from the parking lot before you go in, "Hey wait up. Want to go out!"

I suggest waiting until right after the service. Most people tend to be more open and extra friendly. You might get a chance there where you normally wouldn't.

Standing in line at the Post Office

Free Places to Meet LIVE Woman

Comments:

My friend Chris told me he once had a nice conversation with a hot chick at the post office. She did "web design."

What a coincidence!!! He was looking for a new design for his... web site. He did great at conversation. Too bad he didn't have the balls to ask for her number.

Instead he said, "I'll hit you on Facebook." Unfortunately, his wife did as well.

Don't be caught being a W.L.L. (whining-lying-loser) STRIKE!

Hospital Waiting Room

Free Places to Meet LIVE Woman

Comments:

She will be looking for a place to rest her head. ...

Funeral

Free Places to Meet LIVE Woman

Comments:

My favorite section in the newspaper is the obituary section. "So sad a Playboy model's Billionaire husband dies."

Good news is, a hot girl is available and she's loaded. (She may be a murderer but who doesn't like a little excitement?)

99 Cents Store

Comments:

Personally, I would never date a guy I met at a 99 Cents Store, but some of you might appreciate a girl who can understand a good deal.

"Hey, baby you're so gorgeous I will buy you anything in the store. Really, it's on me."

By the way, have you ever run into someone you haven't seen for a long time at the 99 Cent Store? You don't need to say, "Hi how are you doing?" (because it's the 99 Cent Store). He screamed out my name, "Hey Amy!!!" I said, "Do you mind? I didn't speak to you in high school. What makes you think I'd talk to you here? Get away from me and wipe your nose. Tissues are on aisle three."

Dog Park

Comments:

A fabulous way to have girls come up to YOU. Make sure you have one of those little fru fru dogs. Not one of those Basset Hounds. All she needs is another dog drooling and wanting to hump her leg.

Actually, I found a lost dog in my neighborhood. I knocked on the doors of the huge houses I liked.

"Hi! I found this lost dog. Is the Lady of the house home? No. Well, do you want one?"

The Animal Shelter

Free Places to Meet LIVE Woman

Comments:

Claim, oh how you'd like to rescue them *all* and save the world...bla bla bla.

I met a guy like the above and then he told me he owned a Korean Restaurant TMI (too much information)!

Traffic

Comments:

I know women that have told me they have dated guys this way. To me they are desperate and creepy, but hey I figure it's good for you to know they are out there.

The Gym

Note: #1) Make sure your outfit is not cuter then hers.

#2) Don't make an obvious lies that later will make her feel unsafe.

Comments:

A friendly elderly (near death) and "married" dude sparked up a conversation with me.

I felt he was safe to chat with until he yelled at me for not calling him back one day when he left a message saying he was "suddenly getting a divorce."

(Oh I'm sorry I not into sleeping with guys who, are abusive and are old enough to be my father, BUT I believe Mackenzie Phillips expressed a fancy.)

He said, "Oh are you a Cougar and just like younger guys." I said," Not necessarily, I'm just not into dating an ANGRY, Sabertooth."

The Beach

Chapter 6:

Answers To Questions Guys Want To Know Now!

The Most Frequent Questions Asked

Amy, I want to know now...

Does *size* really matter?

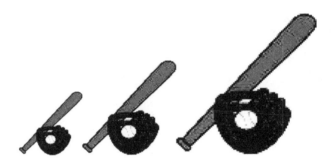

Answer: Yes, size matters.

However, there is a myth that all girls like "big ones." If a girl is small she might prefer a smaller size. The point is girls come in different sizes, too. There is nothing greater than a perrrfect fit. If the glove fits you can't e-quit.

If you are feeling like you don't quite have what it takes to play it doesn't mean you are out of the game. Some girls will accept you bringing other talents or generosity to the plate.

How to Score With a Girl, By a Girl

Amy, I want to know now...

Why will a girl lead you on, just to let you down?

Answers to Questions Guys Want To Know Now!

Answer: The same reason guys do it. (So many reasons so little time.)

1) To get what they want.
2) Don't want to hurt your feelings.
3) Don't want to hear your pleading.
4) YOU are too aggressive and they don't want to deal with it.
5) They are evil, a power trip and like having someone need them.
6) Simply something better came along.

Amy, I want to know now...

What is the best way to get a girl alone when she is out with a pack of her overprotective friends?

Answers to Questions Guys Want To Know Now!

Answer: It was one of the best ways a guy ever asked me out. I was out with several friends of mine. He offered me and one of my friends a drink and then he said, "I would like to talk with you more but see you are busy with your friends. Could I take you to dinner some time? He was the one that was specific after he asked the best time to reach me for a follow up call to make plans.

He was so gracious so he got a chance. (He was hot too…)

Amy, I want to know now...

How do I know when to go in for the kill (sex)?

Answers To Questions Guys Want To Know Now!

Answer: Generally, if a girl moves closer to you, touches you, she may be interested. Give her room and put yourself in a position and location so she can. If she is interested she will. Now if she is constantly doing this in places where you can't go any further, she is probably just flirting or a tease (waste of time...tick-tock).

Let her know, no more teasing. Next time she better put out OR bring someone who will.

(Thanks for the dinners and now I'd like to introduce you to my friend).

"How to Score with a Girl, By a Girl

Amy, I want to know now...

How do you tell when a girl's orgasm is authentic?

Answer: If you have to ask, then it most likely wasn't.

Don't let this bother you too much. That might not be the reason she is with you (even if it's the only reason you are with her). You may be giving her other things she needs. And besides, she can always get that from someone else...ouch!

Ok, now you might consider that dirty word, *communicate*.

Amy, I want to know now...

When you first meet a girl in a bar situation, what is a common lie girls tell that guys may not know?

Answers To Questions Guys Want To Know Now!

Answer: Besides age, weight, and that she used to be a Man...

(Oyyy, women might disown me from our gender) It's the "Birthday Drink." If she is not carrying at least one wrapped present or wearing pink, she's probably just saying it to get a free drink.

You know how some guys play a game to see how many numbers they can get, that they never intend to use? Well, some girls (bitches) play the same game with how many drinks they can get different guys to buy.

Amy, I want to know now...

I am so confused, what is it that most girls look for when it comes to a relationship?

Answers To Questions Guys Want To Know Now!

Answer: Screw them good, buy them stuff or send someone who can.

...Besides that I believe other things most girls want are security, attention, and don't underestimate making them feel good about themselves. Everyone wants to feel special.

Chapter 7:

Best and Worst Pick Up Lines Men Used On Me

Guy's pick up line: "Hey, want to go out. I own a Law firm. "

Amy: "Aw, too bad; I need a root canal. Do you know any Dentists?"

ORRRR maybe a Miner from Chile with a good life insurance policy. I hear they make a lot of money, go away for long periods of time and have a short life expectancy.

On second thought let me have your number I'll file it away for when I go to Chile and need an Attorney...not.

(I needed a lawyer to rep me for a TV deal. Geez, ended up needing a lawyer to rep me for my lawyer that was representing me!)

(A "brilliant" comic)

Guy's pick up line: "Hey do you mind if I pick you up?" (And then he tries to literally pick me up off the ground.)

Best and Worst Pick Up Lines Men Used

Amy: "Not if you don't mind if I hit on you." (as I sock him in the gut).

Guy's pick up line: "My fantasy is when one of these days I walk you down the aisle."

Amy: "LOL. Excuse me but you ARE married!

(Continue…)

(Continued)

Guy's pick up line: "The aisle of Bank of America when we deposit your check from the TV show I get you."

Comment:

Well that was a good one. He got me!!!

(Actually, it ended up I got myself a TV show and he got a divorce.)

Guy's pick up line: Want to come up to my house in the Hills and see my art and drink some wine?

Best and Worst Pick Up Lines Men Used

Amy:

"Wow OMG! I should set you up with my mother!
She is an artist, loves wine and you seem like a real
Mother F@cker."

Guy's pick up line: (As I am engrossed in a deep conversation with a friend he interrupts and says...)

"Hey, I want to dance with you."

Amy:

Oh thank you, not now, I'm in a discussion with a friend here.

Guy's pick up line:

But really I want to dance right NOW!

(Continue...)

Amy:

(...Continued)

Amy:

Then maybe you should do the Hokey Pokey and turn yourself around.

Guy's pick up line: "One of these nights I'd like to follow you home and attack you."

Best and Worst Pick Up Lines Men Used

Amy: OK! Let me check my calendar.

I'm sorry Charles Manson had a better approach than you. (STRIKE! And too bad, was definitely attracted.)

How to Score With a Girl, By a Girl

Guy's pick up line:

I'd like to go back to your house and have a threesome.

Best and Worst Pick Up Lines Men Used

Amy:

"Great, at my house, my idea of a threesome is one guy is cleaning my house and the other is fixing my computer."

Comment:

Forget emotional support. I'm looking for technical support. I need some ram and a hacker with a HUGE HARD drive.

Chapter 8:

Things Girls Want Guys to Know Now!...

—

(After interviewing many girls)

How to Score With a Girl, By a Girl

"Don't consider your 'text' as a form of communication if you want to get a response, especially after first meeting or date."

(Pick up the phone!)

"Don't put your fingers in your mouth."

"If your breath smells, don't breathe."

"Don't tell a girl the truth if she does look fat in those jeans or if you do want to sleep with her sister."

"Make sure your teeth are white or buy Crest White Strips."

"Gifts of clothes and jewelry rather than candy and flowers with get you further faster."

"Don't say you'll call if you won't."

"Don't talk about old girlfriends."

Things Girls Want Guys to Know Now...

"DON'T talk to us in a restaurant if we have bought our meal and just started eating it."

"Make sure your clothes are clean."

"Don't let a girl pay for the date."

"Don't yell or cuss."

"Listen, give attention."

"Be gracious."

"Refrain from giving noticeable attention to other girls when you are with the girl you want to score with."

"Don't give us what YOU want. Give us what WE want and we'll give you what YOU want. "

If you are not good at sex, spending money or doing stuff for us... send someone who can.

How to Score With a Girl, By a Girl

"Act happy,confident and empowering. "

"Offer something to make her feel good about herself." (Note: a good way to attract anyone.)

Oh, yeah and some girls like... being treated like sh*t

See next Chapter, "If All Else Fails Be a Jerk."

Chapter 9:
If All Else Fails Be a Jerk

How to Score With a Girl, By a Girl

This is the old story where you build her self-esteem just to bring her down.

Just remember, "Crazy is as crazy does."

I know plenty of men that do this one and always end up alone and complain how their last girlfriend was "psycho."

No, let's say it together guys... "You chose a girlfriend who was psycho." That's ok if that's your thing. Just remember that's what YOU were fishing for. If you ask for it, you will get it. And you most likely won't like what you get.

For you "jerks" out there refer back to

Chapter: #2, "Know Your Category," section "Ads for the Internet to Attract Dumb Gold Diggers".

(A little something for everyone).

Chapter 10:

"Practice" to Consistently Score

(Remember there is lots of Practice and playing before winning the World Series)

Exercises to help you successfully approach a girl and start a successful conversation to assure scoring. How do I approach a girl or say the perfect opening line?

Exercise #1 For one week practice with girls you are NOT interested in. "What?" you say. Especially the ones you are NOT interested in. It's all about being in the moment, listening so you can connect, and most of all, your **intent**

You and I already know your intent is to get a home run ASAP. You should hide this from girls so they don't feel you are on the hunt or being nice for an ulterior motive which can be hard to do, so that is why I suggest practicing with all types you don't want..

What is the best opening line?

I went over this earlier. Find something positive to say about the girl. Just relax and remember she is a human being and give her a compliment. That's it! It could be anything from saying, "You have pretty hair" to" That's a gorgeous color on you." And then keep walking. "What?" you say.

Yes, keep walking. Your only purpose is to give a compliment and not expect anything back. Make the girl feel good without expecting anything in return. Practice this for the week.

Exercise #2 Week #2

Combine Exercise #1 and Exercise#2

Open with a compliment, but if she responds and tells you something, listen and expand. Ask her a couple of questions about what she just told you. You will come across sincerely interested in her and she will start to emotionally trust you. Score!

If a girl opens up and you haven't listened and gone to another subject she will think you are really not interested in her inner qualities...or you are an idiot.

Practice this so when you meet the person that makes you feel you just like put your hand in an electrical socket, you will have practiced these techniques and hopefully increased your chances of not f@@king it up.

When you are relaxed and not attached to the results, you will usually start getting what you want (as in anything in life). It's kind of like; have you ever heard a guy say, "I can't believe it now that I'm attached or committed to someone I finally have girls coming on to me all the time."

Believe it or not the above will allow for the fastest way to score with girls...and people.

How to Score With a Girl, By a Girl

And don't forget once you have made a connection to

    a) Ask her a specific thing she likes (sushi, rollerblading, hang gliding)

    b) When you get her phone number give her a choice of best time to call to make plans (next day, beginning of week, etc.).

Now that you've been to practice it's time to start the game. Good luck! And remember. You lose some, win some, and if not turn the book over and look at the cover. ☺

Best to you, good luck and see you on the field!